ARE YOU A PROPHET

ENCOURAGING YOU TO ANSWER THE CALL AND PREPARING TO SOAR

THE TEACHER'S EDITION

MALINDA M. HARRIS

LAKEVIEW
PUBLICATIONS

No part of this book may be used or reproduced by any means, graphic, electronic, or mechanical, including photocopying, recording, taping or by any information storage retrieval system without the written permission of the publisher except for the use of brief quotations in a book review. Copying this book is both illegal and unethical.

Copyright © 2023 Malinda Marie Harris
All rights reserved.
Published by: LakeView Publications
Cover by: Bobby Barnhill
Layout by: Craig & Amanda Price
Edited by: LakeView Publications

Eagle's Emerge
Rise up!

ARE YOU A PROPHET

ENCOURAGING YOU TO ANSWER THE CALL AND PREPARING TO SOAR

THE TEACHER'S EDITION

MALINDA M. HARRIS

The ESV® Bible (The Holy Bible, English Standard Version®). ESV® Text Edition: 2016. Copyright © 2001 by Crossway, a publishing ministry of Good News Publishers. The ESV® text has been reproduced in cooperation with and by permission of Good News Publishers. Unauthorized reproduction of this publication is prohibited. All rights reserved.

New American Standard Bible®, Copyright © 1960, 1971, 1977, 1995, 2020 by The Lockman Foundation. All rights reserved.

THE HOLY BIBLE, NEW INTERNATIONAL VERSION®, NIV® Copyright © 1973, 1978, 1984, 2011 by Biblica, Inc.® Used by permission. All rights reserved worldwide.

Scripture quotations from The Authorized (King James) Version. Rights in the Authorized Version in the United Kingdom are vested in the Crown. Reproduced by permission of the Crown's patentee, Cambridge University Press.

Scripture taken from the Good News Translation in Today's English Version-Second Edition Copyright © 1992 by American Bible Society. Used by Permission.

Copyright © 2015 by The Lockman Foundation, La Habra, CA 90631. All rights reserved. For Permission To Quote information visit http://www.lockman.org/ The "Amplified" trademark is registered in the United States Patent and Trademark Office by The Lockman Foundation. Use of this trademark requires the permission of The Lockman Foundation.

Scripture taken from the New King James Version®. Copyright © 1982 by Thomas Nelson. Used by permission. All rights reserved.

Holy Bible, New Living Translation, copyright © 1996, 2004, 2015 by Tyndale House Foundation. Used by permission of Tyndale House Publishers, Inc., Carol Stream, Illinois 60188. All rights reserved.

American Standard Version (ASV) is Public Domain.

CONTENTS

Acknowledgments — ix
Introduction — xi

1. Identity — 1
2. The Office of a Prophet is Not Only for Men but for Women as Well! — 19
3. Are You a Prophet? — 31
4. Prepare for Warfare — 43
5. The Call — 59
6. Breaking off the Spirit of Self-Rejection — 71
7. Unshakeable Faith — 81
8. Dig Deeper — 95
9. Trust is a Key — 105
10. A Prophetic Word for What is to Come! — 117

Afterword — 133
About the Author — 135
About the Publisher — 137

This book is dedicated to all the emerging prophets and prophetic voices across the United States and globally. I pray this book lights a new fire, fresh wind and refocus each and everyone of you to pursue God like never before to step into your calling, purpose, and destiny without reservation, hesitation or second-guessing what God has called you to do!

ACKNOWLEDGMENTS

This journey in my life has been exciting and full of lessons that I am honored to share with great people who are family. Writing this book by far has been the hardest part of this journey. All the support, friendship, and love are what gave me the strength and encouragement to finish strong in writing this book.

I want to thank:

My Family for being a supportive force in me accomplishing my dreams!

My Isaiah 61 Ministry family! I love you all!

I want to thank God most of all, without God, this wouldn't be possible!

INTRODUCTION

RIVERS OF LIVING WATER

He that believeth on me, as the scripture hath said, from within him shall flow rivers of living water.

— JOHN 7:38 ASV

This teacher's guide book was written with you, the educator, and your God-given calling in mind. My passion and heart's cry is to use my testimony to help your students firmly establish their identity in Christ. I pray that God, through this work, will teach them how to answer their call so they can become more confident in exercising their divine purpose.

Through my life's experiences, trials, and tribulations, I hope your students will discover that they are not alone in

INTRODUCTION

their setbacks, setups, and disappointments. These challenges are the vehicles by which God delivers them to the place He created them to thrive in. Remember, each and every one of us has an inner well filled with living waters, waiting to flow out of us to help train, equip, and build one another up to accomplish and fulfill our destinies on earth.

My hope in writing this book is to encourage, uplift, and bring confirmation and peace to every reader. I pray that your students will apply the different steps and scriptures to each area of their lives and that God will pull out the best in them so that they will walk in full victory over every circumstance and situation that has tried to hinder them from stepping into their calling.

To assist you in facilitating these life-changing lessons, each chapter includes a detailed lesson plan breakdown of the concepts and ideas presented. This outline provides a framework for your instruction and offers space for you to personalize it to fit the specific needs and learning styles of your students.

IDENTITY

For we are his workmanship, created in Christ Jesus for good works, which God prepared beforehand, that we should walk in them.

— EPHESIANS 2:10 ESV

"Alright everyone, it's movie night!" I remember being excited about movie night with my siblings. The smell of movie popcorn with extra butter filled the kitchen and the den. We were excited to watch scary movies that my mom rented for us from the video store. I can remember watching three movies that night with my siblings. We usually went straight to bed when we felt sleepy, but for some reason, this night, we all passed out on the couch. I do not remember anyone picking us up two by two and carrying us up the stairs. However, I do remember being woken up to being touched inappropriately between my legs. I started crying and I woke-up hitting him in the face and yelled "STOP IT!!! Mom help!!!"

My mother came flying out of her room yelling, *"Hey! Put them Down Now! They are too big for you to be carrying. Next time wake them up!"* I was eleven years old when I started experiencing sexual abuse by my stepdad.

The molestation from my step-dad started on that day, and it went on until I was fourteen years of age. I was offered alcohol as he would try to French kiss me and was told, "This is how your Husband will kiss you one day."

Once, while I was taking a bath, he was standing at the door watching me bathe. My grandmother caught him and almost took his head off with her baseball bat. After that situation, my mom put locks on the bathroom door and my bedroom door as well. Even in spite of all the warning signs, my mom would go out on the weekends, leaving us at home with him. He would come into my room after everyone else was sleeping, and molest me. He would throw money at me when he was done. I was so afraid to tell anyone what I was going through. I was told that no one would believe me because he was paying me for a service, as if I was a prostitute.

One Sunday morning we were all getting ready for church, and he had hidden my shoes and my mom was fussing at me to find them. She was in such a hurry she left me at home with him. This was the first time he forced me to have sex with him. I could remember crying and blaming myself for what had happened. I thought if I were stronger I could have fought him off. I felt so dirty and ashamed. I just wanted to go into hiding and never come out. It was a time of crushing darkness. I retreated so far into myself that I pushed everyone away – friends, family, everyone. I was utterly alone.

Summer nights were filled with the drone of my stepdad and his friend's drunken conversations on the porch. Their voices would rise and fall, punctuated by the clinking of beer bottles. Their conversations, usually about work or sports, would sometimes veer into uncomfortable territory – "casing out the young girls" as they put it. It made my skin crawl.

One evening, Sarah, my friend from down the street, wandered over. The men started their usual routine, showering her with unwanted compliments. I knew exactly where this was headed. "Don't listen," I warned her, my voice tight. "They just want to take advantage." Sarah, however, brushed it off, her teenage naiveté shining through.

The tension escalated quickly. When one of the men lunged toward Sarah, she reacted fiercely. A swift kick to a very sensitive area sent him yelping and clutching himself. Sarah wasted no time, disappearing into the twilight like a shot. Laughter bubbled up from inside me, a welcome release from the simmering anger. It was short-lived. The man I'd just mocked whipped around, rage contorting his face. My moment of triumph became a scramble to avoid a beating as my mom rushed in, demanding answers.

One night, the familiar creak of the connecting door shattered the silence. He stood there, half-naked, a predator sizing up his prey. Years of abuse boiled over. Without a word, I reached under my pillow, my fingers finding the cold steel of two butcher knives. Crossing them over his crotch, I held them steady, the glint a silent threat. The air crackled with unspoken words.

My voice, hoarse with a mix of fear and defiance, ripped through the darkness. "This ends now. You ever come in here again, asking for 'it' or anything else, and I won't hesitate."

The journal, a silent witness to countless nights, lay open on the nightstand. I shoved it at him, along with a pen. A promise, scrawled on that page, was the only thing keeping those blades from finding their mark.

That next day my stepdad picked a fight with my mom about me and said that "she *will have to go, or I we will leave.*" My mom chose him over me. I went to school the next day and spoke with my track coach. He told me he knew of a safe place I could go and stay until I could figure out what I was going to do. I stayed at a safe haven for a few months before moving in with my aunt and became so depressed that I swallowed a hand full of pills. I wanted to end my life.

I was shuffled once again, this time to my dad's house. Where I became Cinderella. I was living in a nightmare. A dream that felt like I would never come out of. My father was diagnosed with multiple sclerosis when he was 18 years old, and it began effecting his body in his mid to late 20 or early 30's. He was disabled, and he was very disgruntled when I moved in. He had good days and bad days. I became a real-life Cinderella at sixteen. I had to clean, cook, babysit, and be a caregiver for my father while going to high school. I also worked a part-time job. I can remember sitting on my bed asking God to help me through this tough time in my life. I wish I could say I had a prince come and rescue me, but I cannot.

I can remember being in my darkest state when I saw different color orbs in the air and as they busted, I could hear different voices say, kill yourself, no one cares anyway, they don't want you and so on and so forth. I knew in my heart that the enemy was trying to destroy any remaining identity I had. Going through the trauma of sexual abuse destroys a person's identity.

The enemy comes by any means necessary to steal, kill, and destroy the seed that has been planted down on the inside of us by God.

The attacks come to abort the purpose, plans, and destiny that has been planted in a person with a high calling. It does this by stripping the person of his or her identity. You will not know who you are and whom you belong to, just like Adam and Eve.

When they fell in the garden, they no longer saw themselves as God saw them or how God identified them to be. This causes us to hide ourselves in shame, rejection, and self-pity. It opens the door to depression, self-hatred, and even suicide. By allowing these open doors to the enemy, he can come in like a flood to minister to our thoughts, reactions, and emotions.

Some things that the enemy will minister to our thoughts are that we are not good enough and no one will ever truly love us. This lie, once believed, can lead us down two divergent paths, both equally destructive.

The Path of Promiscuity: Believing ourselves undeserving of genuine love, some may seek validation through fleeting physical intimacy. Jumping from relationship to relationship becomes a desperate attempt to fill the void within. However, this constant seeking only deepens the wounds, leaving them perpetually raw and unhealed.

The Path of Prude: Others, fearing the vulnerability required for intimacy, may retreat behind a wall of prudishness. This suppression, while seemingly offering protection, can open the door to a different kind of bondage – addiction. Drowning the pain in substances, reckless behavior, or isolating oneself become substitutes for genuine connection, leaving them trapped in a self-made prison.

The raw truth is, if you never sit steal and truly deal with the root of the issue at hand, this can cause a major detour from the destiny, plan, and purpose God has preordained and predestined for our lives.

The detour causes a demonic cycle that needs to be broken off between us and our generations past, present, and future. Once you stand up flat footed and take a stand, you can break the demonic cycles and remove the demonic banners and labels that the enemy has clothed you in your life.

Friends, there's a real battle going on in the spiritual realm. It can be a struggle when you start to close the doors to negativity and doubt. But remember, the true enemy is satan, not the people who might be influenced by him. Those closest to us can sometimes be used as instruments, but the real enemy is satan, the source of those lies and negativity.

Some of the lies spoken over me were that I would never get married or have children and if I did marry, my husband was going to control me and I would never have a voice or be heard. I would never amount to anything, I wasn't good enough, I was a prostitute and had been paid for sex. Alcohol was presented to me as a way to forget my part in my feelings, and was a promise to make me feel better.

Have you ever been made to feel you are worthless and dirty? I cannot help but wonder how many other people have gone through similar trauma and blame themselves for being molested. Do you feel you are in a cycle year after year? Is it hard for you to trust again? Do you know your worth?

After going through personal ministry and counseling, it hit me like a ton of bricks. The person was a vessel yielding to demonic oppression and deception due them being spiritually dead and living for the world and its ruler the devil or Satan.

If we look at the person as being in a broken state this will help us in the process of forgiving them as the father has forgiven us.

> *Be kind to one another, compassionate,*
> *forgiving each other, just as God in*
> *Christ also has forgiven you.*
>
> — EPHESIANS 4:32 NASB

Know that you are not alone, and you do not have to suffer in silence any longer. You can find your voice and identity in Christ Jesus. Once we come out of agreement with the enemy and the lies that we have believed that has been spoken over our lives through fear tactics and intimidation, we find hope in Christ and what he did for us in the cross through his redemptive power and resurrection power. We expect who we are through Christ Jesus and his blood washes us white as snow and gives us hope and a clean slate. It's like the 12 disciples before they became apostles. They had to sit at Jesus' feet and learn who they were and how to operate in their true identity. God is not a respecter of person. God intends for all people to find their identity in Christ. If you're a Christian, your identity encompasses all the abundance of being a beloved child of God.

WHAT IS IDENTITY?

Identity means the fact of being who or what a person or thing is.

Identity also means the condition of being oneself or itself, and not another.

Another definition of identity is condition or character as to who a person or what a thing is; the qualities, beliefs, etc., that distinguish or identify a person or thing. The definition I love is the state or fact of being the same one as described. God has described our identity of who we are in his word. Knowing that you are a child of God and what has been spoken and stated about you allows us to identify who God says that we are.

Here's how you can start living your life fully in Christ, keeping in mind that your identity is found in Jesus Christ.

FOURTEEN THINGS THAT GOD HAS SAID ABOUT YOU AND YOUR IDENTITY IN CHRIST:

*1. **YOU ARE A SAINT** - The fact that you've placed your trust in Jesus Christ is enough to qualify you to be a saint. Even though you'll still struggle with sin while you live in this fallen world, your core identity as a Christian is as a saint, not a sinner – and you can always count on Jesus' help to overcome sin in your life.*
*2. **YOU ARE BLESSED** - God has given you the greatest blessing of all – Himself.*
*3. **YOU ARE APPRECIATED** - God notices and appreci-*

ates every good choice you make throughout your life – even when other people don't.

4. YOU ARE SAVED - Thanks to Jesus' sacrifice on the cross, you're saved from: sin, death, Satan, your old human nature, and a pattern of worldly living.

5. YOU ARE RECONCILED - Jesus has spiritually reconciled you to God and other believers.

6. YOU ARE AFFLICTED - Everyone in this fallen world – Christians and non-Christians alike – must endure suffering. However, as a Christian, your suffering can accomplish good, redemptive purposes.

> *Take My yoke upon you and learn from Me;*
> *for I am gentle and humble in heart, and*
> *you will find rest for your souls. For my*
> *yolk is easy and my burden is light.*
>
> — MATTHEW 11:30

7. YOU ARE HEARD - God always hears and responds to your prayers when you're connected to Him through Jesus.

8. YOU ARE GIFTED - God has given you special abilities that He wants you to use in the Christian ministry He calls you to – both inside church, and out in your community.

9. YOU ARE NEW - Jesus placed a new spirit within you when you began a relationship with Him.

***10. YOU ARE FORGIVEN** - You can thank Jesus for forgiving you by obeying His commands to forgive others who have harmed you and to seek forgiveness from people you've harmed.*
__11. YOU ARE ADOPTED__ - you've been adopted into God's family.
__12. YOU ARE LOVED__ - God's love is perfect.
__13. YOU ARE REWARDED__ - God will reward you for everything faithful and holy that you do as a Christian.
__14. YOU ARE VICTORIOUS__ - Jesus has given you the power to ultimately overcome evil, sin, and death. (Use the spiritual weapons at your disposal as a Christian truth, righteousness, the Gospel, faith, salvation, scripture, prayer, and the strength to stand in spiritual battles, trusting that you can always emerge victorious.)

This is the reason why the bible tells us to give our testimony so that God can do it again and again. You have to know who you are and who's you are.

What God delivered me from, He can deliver you from too! You will see the demonic cycles broken off of your life as you receive the truth about who you are in Jesus Christ and what God has already spoken about you.

That's the good news which gives us hope to stand on as you walk through your process and journey with God rediscovering who you are. Remember...they have gained the victory over him (the enemy) because of the blood of the Lamb and of the testimony which they have borne. Revelations 12:11

HAVE YOU ACCEPTED YOUR IDENTITY IN CHRIST JESUS?

These are just some things to meditate on in your free time of reflecting on what you have read in each chapter. Feel free to journal the answers so that you can go back and see where God had brought you in your journey with him.

MEDITATION FOR THOUGHT:

1. *What does Identity mean to you?*
2. *Do you identify with who God has described that you are? (If not why?)*
3. *When is the last time that you stood up and given a testimony of the goodness of God and what you have overcome through Christ Jesus?*

_____

_____

_____

_____

_____

_____

_____

_____

Identity in Christ Jesus

Introduction

- **Scripture:** Ephesians 2:10
- **Thesis:** Our identity is found in Christ Jesus, and understanding this truth can lead to healing, freedom, and a fulfilling life.

i. **The Importance of Identity**
    - **The Impact of Lies:** Negative beliefs can hinder our growth and relationship with God.
    - **The Cycle of Demonic Influence:** Unresolved trauma can lead to generational curses.
    - **The Battle for the Mind:** Satan attacks our identity to keep us from fulfilling God's purpose.

ii. **Discovering Our True Identity**
    - **The Broken State of Humanity:** We need forgiveness and healing.
    - **The Power of Forgiveness:** Following God's example of forgiveness can lead to freedom.
    - **The Importance of Self-Love:** Recognizing our worth is crucial to breaking free from negative cycles.

iii. **Identity in Christ Jesus**
   - **Understanding Identity:** Defining identity and its significance.
   - **God's Description of Us:** Fourteen attributes that reveal our true identity in Christ.
   - **The Power of Testimony:** Sharing our stories can inspire others and glorify God.
iv. **Living Fully in Christ**
   - **Accepting Our Identity:** Embracing the truth of who we are in Christ.
   - **Breaking Free from Lies:** Overcoming negative beliefs and embracing God's truth.
   - **Experiencing Freedom and Healing:** The transformative power of living in Christ.

QUESTIONS FOR THE CLASS:

1. What does Identity mean to you?
2. Do you identify with who God has described that you are? (If not why?)
3. When is the last time that you stood up and given a testimony of the goodness of God and what you have overcome through Christ Jesus?

ARE YOU A PROPHET

MALINDA M. HARRIS

THE OFFICE OF A PROPHET IS NOT ONLY FOR MEN BUT FOR WOMEN AS WELL!

> *You did not choose me, but I chose you and appointed you so that you might go and bear fruit—fruit that will last—and so that whatever you ask in my name the Father will give you.*
>
> — JOHN 15:16 NIV

Just recently, I was asked to prepare a short teaching on the keys to the prophetic at my church. The weight of expectation settled on my shoulders like a heavy cloak. Leading a teaching session on prophecy for the prayer and prophesy team – my own church family! Nervousness coiled in my gut, a tightening knot that spread like wildfire. Sweat beaded on my forehead, and my carefully prepared words danced out of reach.

Just as I stumbled over a sentence, the room seemed to tilt. My heart hammered a frantic rhythm against my ribs, and the urge to flee threatened to overwhelm me. Then, Pastor's hand gently stopped my flow. Panic surged – had I messed up that badly?

But as I met her gaze, a wave of relief washed over me. A warm smile and a reassuring nod replaced my fear. "Take a breath," her silent message conveyed, "and let's begin again."

My voice trembled slightly as I began the teaching, but I pushed on. The room held its breath – you could practically hear a pin drop. I tried to spark some engagement, tossing out questions about key terms, but the silence remained heavy. Discouragement threatened to pull me under.

Then, I reached a pivotal point – the foundational scripture. As I shared it, a shift seemed to ripple through the room. The ice began to thaw, replaced by a quiet attentiveness. This renewed their focus, and emboldened, I transitioned to the heart of the message – the prophetic revelation God had given me about John 7:38.

I wonder if I were a man, would I have had that level of fear? As a prophetic woman, the level of spiritual attack that comes with sharing a word from the Lord really does go up a notch. Over the years, I have asked myself these questions as the Holy Spirit would unction me to step out and speak the words He has placed in my mouth. It has been a major challenge and hindrance to know that people question your call and tell you that there are no prophets anymore because we are all prophets and can speak over our own lives and hear the voice of God for ourselves. As I spent more time in prayer, the Holy Spirit revealed the real reason behind what was causing me to run and hide. It was coming from one of the major spirits that fights the prophetic voices, which is the spirit of religion.

The spirit of religion and control will have us believe as women, that we are only called to be housewives and mothers. It will have us sit back and take a back seat to our spouses if we are married or sit down and shut up, as many men and leaders refer to the scriptures that have been taken out of contexts for many centuries and decades. Let us look at things from God's perspective and not from our belief system or manmade laws and regulations.

God's hand has been on my life in a powerful way, guiding me towards becoming a prophet. It's an ongoing journey of transformation. The more I surrender to His process, the more He shapes me for this calling.

There are many women God has used in the bible, who stood in the office of a prophet or prophetess.

What is a prophet? A prophet is a divine functionary who serves as the spokesperson for God. What is a prophetess? A prophetess is a female prophet.

Female prophets have the same ascribed power, authority, and competences as their male counterparts do. The bible names these ladies as female prophets Deborah, Huldah, Miriam, Sarah, Anna, Philip's daughters.

If we go and look in the bible and see where God said that I will pour out my spirit on all people. Joel 2:28, Isaiah 44:3, Acts 2:17 and Romans 5:5 This is a large key, to the prophetic, that people easily miss.

God is calling the woman forth in this season to speak, "Thus says the Lord." We are being called out of the background to the forefront. God has called us to stand side by side to our male counterparts. God is calling us out of the shadows of our spouses, boyfriends, or controlling leaders in this season. He has already prepared the pathways for us to move forward in him and his calling that he has placed on our lives.

The Holy Spirit, showed through the children of Israel's experience with pharaoh, that there are many pharaohs in today's church and ministries that have oppressed women from doing anything besides choir, children's ministry, church daycare, serving in the kitchen, usher/greeter ministry, dance ministry, or reading the announcements.

I want to clarify when I say pharaoh, is its pertaining to the spirit and motives behind why a ministry will not allow woman to come forth. It is a mindset rooted in the spirit of religion or a false belief system. Don't worry or be concerned because God is delivering us just as he delivered the children of Israel from their pharaoh. He is moving in the exact same way today to deliver us from the pharaohs in our Churches, ministries and even our jobs or marketplace ministries. We must continue to look up and keep our focus on the father and yield to his leadership and guidance in this season and seasons to come.

We are being called to Arise, Arise in this season. Step into the place that the Lord has called us to as female prophets. We have the power and authority of Jesus Christ to step out and speak the words that God has placed down on the inside of us.

God is taking us from the boat, shore, cave, and the mountains to soar with him and proclaim the word of Lord and stand in boldness in the midst of opposition and declare the exceptional day of the Lord. Speak his precepts and obey no matter what is looks like. He is calling us to speak to the dry bones, as Ezekiel did.

God is calling us to decree and declare the song of the Lord like Deborah did. He is calling us to be that General of God, to operate in the seven spirits of God like Deborah, Huldah,

Miriam, Sarah, Anna, Philip's daughters. We shall move in the supernatural and creative power of God.

God is calling us to rise up in our faith and trust in him and stand tall and strong in his boldness. Now is the time, now is the season to put your hand to the plow and press forward like an ox strong, and steady with power in the Lord.

Now is the time not to shrink back but to step out on God's words that he placed before you. Now is the time to reach up to heaven and pull down the strategies that God's people need to build the things that God said that needs to be pulled from heaven down to earth. Now is the time stand, dig in your heels and not be moved or shaken. The time has come to reclaim what's rightfully yours! Let's approach the heart of the Father with unwavering faith. Petition Him to overturn those court cases the enemy has tried to use against you. Don't just seek dismissal; ask God to turn this situation around in your favor, to bless you with double the victory you deserve!

Ladies, when you step out and yield to your process, you will see the hand of God move mightily, not only on your behalf but on the behalf, of others and accomplish the word that it was set out to achieve.

Over the years I have been through trials, good times, and bad times but through it all I can say that I have truly enjoyed my transition from dancing prophetically to being a mouthpiece of God, to training, teaching, and equipping up and coming prophetic voice and prophets. Just as I yielded to my process, you will need to yield to your own process.

I was once told that I was holding up others who needed to come up behind me because I didn't want to go through the process any longer. But, through prayer and fasting and a lot of self-evaluation I repented and continue to yield to my process.

As I yielded, I saw all kinds of doors open for me. Once I let go and let God, everything began to rapidly shift.

I want to encourage you to trust God and give him all the difficult places, allow the Holy Spirit to pull you through, and use the hidden things to show you where God can still use those places to glorify Him.

Do not be concerned about what people might think or feel. Take God's hand and allow him to breathe life into the dead and dry, dark places of your soul. Allow God to enlarge your territory so that you can hold the capacity of anointing, glory, and power-God wants to pour into you.

MEDITATION FOR THOUGHT:

1. *What God planted strategies, plans, or blueprints have you been sitting on?*
2. *And what have you done with those God given dreams?*
3. *When is the last time you took God's hand and allowed Him to breathe life into the dead areas that have been hidden, put on the shelf, or disregarded?*
4. *Has God been calling you to Arise, Arise, and Shine in this season?*

_____

_____

_____

_____

_____

_____

_____

_____

_____

The Rise of Female Prophets

Introduction

- **Scripture:** John 15:16
- **Thesis:** Women are called to the prophetic office and have the same authority and power as male prophets.

i. **The Prophetic Calling**
   - **The Nature of Prophecy:** A divine function of speaking for God.
   - **The Biblical Examples:** Women prophets throughout history (Deborah, Huldah, Miriam, Sarah, Anna, Philip's daughters).
   - **The Call to All People:** God's promise to pour out His Spirit on all flesh.

ii. **Overcoming Obstacles**
   - **Pharaohs in the Church:** False beliefs and religious mindsets that hinder women's leadership.
   - **The Deliverance of God:** God's power to break free from oppressive forces.
   - **The Call to Arise:** A challenge to step into the prophetic role.

iii. **The Power and Authority of Female Prophets**

- ○ **The Seven Spirits of God:** The supernatural abilities granted to female prophets.
  - ○ **The Boldness of Faith:** Standing firm in the face of opposition.
  - ○ **The Declaring of God's Word:** Proclaiming God's message with confidence.
- iv. **Yielding to the Process**
  - ○ **The Journey of Transformation:** Personal growth and development necessary for prophetic ministry.
  - ○ **Letting Go and Letting God:** Surrendering to God's guidance and timing.
  - ○ **The Rewards of Obedience:** The blessings and fulfillment that come from following God's call.

QUESTIONS FOR THE CLASS:

1. What God planted strategies, plans, or blueprints have you been sitting on?
2. And what have you done with them those God given dreams?
3. When is the last time you took God's hand and allowed Him to breathe life into the dead areas that have been hidden, put on the shelf, or disregarded?

4. Has God been calling you to Arise, Arise, and Shine in this season?

_____
_____
_____
_____
_____
_____
_____
_____
_____
_____
_____
_____
_____
_____
_____

ARE YOU A PROPHET?

The "prophet" proclaimed the message given to him, as the "seer" beheld the vision of God

— NUMBERS 12:6

The dream within the dream. 10 plus years ago, I had a dream that turned out to be a dream within a dream. On the night of my dream, I was exhausted from the WOW (Woman of the Word Conference).

Something strange had happened to me during the worship service. I was worshipping, and words started coming out of my mouth. As I spoke, people were falling out behind me in the spirit. I could feel a wave washing over people and then the music stopped. I could hear our Pastor say, "The

Prophet has spoken the word of the Lord." I was confounded at what had just taken place. As I prepared to lay down that evening I remember hearing a phone ring, but it was not a natural phone. It was a spiritual phone, accompanied by an angel telling me the Lord wanted to speak with me. As I fell to sleep, I saw Jesus standing at the foot of my bed and he was speaking to my Pastors at that time. It was interesting that different Apostles, Pastors, Prophets, Teachers, and Evangelist appeared in my bedroom 2 by 2 inquiring of who I AM.

I remember having a dream within a dream. I dreamt Jesus was speaking to me and them simultaneously. Jesus was explaining to me, they were questioning him about my calling and if I was called to their Church or not, and was I a prophet? or not? The leaders were asking the Lord if I was called to dance prophetically, oversee, or instruct?

Jesus answered their questions as He was speaking to me, confirming to me those temporary things are coming to an end. "I AM calling you fourth to speak the words I have placed down on the inside of you. I have equipped you to train my up-and-coming prophets. I have called you as a Samuel, but you will experience different seasons like Deborah, Elijah, Daniel, Joseph and many more."

Jesus touched my mouth and it was like a hot coal had been placed in my mouth and down my throat. Then I woke-up.

I received a text message from our pastors requesting to meet with me about transitioning from being over the dance ministry. A few days before my meeting, I attended a prophetic prayer meeting with a few friends and family. We worshipped and listened as a Prophet started calling people out of the crowd. As he looked around the room my body felt as though it had caught on fire, and I heard a voice in the spirit that declared, "You're next."

The Prophet called me up and asked my name and then he started prophesying to me. He confirmed I was transitioning, the scriptures God had been speaking to me, and that I was studying were exactly as my dream had declared. This was one way that God confirmed my calling. The other way was through taking to scripture confirming who I am in Him and what he has called me to. I was nervous to step out in this new adventure with the Lord.

Do you feel that you are called to be or become a Prophet? Has the Lord been tugging at your heart to step out in your calling? Have you ever used excuses not to answer your call? Are you a loaner? Is speaking publicly a struggle or challenge for you? How about your love walk, is it difficult to speak from a place of grace, mercy, and compassion? Are you to young?

> *Before I formed thee in the belly, I knew thee; and before thou camest forth out of the womb I sanctified thee, and I ordained thee a prophet unto the nations.*
>
> — JEREMIAH 1:5 KJV

LET US LOOK AT JEREMIAH'S CALL IN JEREMIAH 1:6-10:

> *6 Then said I, Ah, Lord God! Behold, I cannot speak: for I am a child.*
> *7 But the Lord said unto me, say not, I am a child: for thou shalt go to all that I shall send thee, and whatsoever I command thee thou shalt speak.*
> *8 Be not afraid of their faces: for I am with thee to deliver thee, saith the Lord.*
> *9 Then the Lord put forth his hand and touched my mouth. And the Lord said unto me, Behold, I have put my words in thy mouth.*
> *10 See, I have this day set thee over the nations and over the kingdoms, to root out, and to pull down, and to destroy, and to throw down, to build, and to plant.*

As we see, God had to shift Jeremiah's perception of how he saw his self. God built Jeremiah's confidence and trust in Him by confirming who Jeremiah was and called to be.

God released Jeremiah into his journey and process by speaking into existence who Jeremiah was already predestined to be in the future by pulling those words into his present state. God went into Jeremiah's book of life and breathed life on what was already written and pulled it into the present time. God will do the same for you. He will speak into existence who you are and what you are called to do in the ministry. God will confirm to you first as He did with Jeremiah and so many of his prophets and mouth pieces.

As we accept the high calling God places on our lives, we will soar to the places our doubts and unbelief cannot live or hold us back. As we take the first step to yielding and obeying God, the Journey begins with the making and building of a prophet. We begin to trust God, the Lord, and the Holy Spirit. Our faith starts to arise, and the fear begins to fall off. The Lord puts His words in our mouths. His words and not our own, but His words. We begin to have the mind of Christ; we see things from God's point of view and not our own. The training begins when he starts to ask us what we see, hear, discern, and know? As we answer correctly and hit the bullseye, we are being prepared to stand and speak, "Thus says the Lord." You must first learn what type of technology you have prophetically. What do I mean by that huh?

The first step is figuring out what kind of prophetic technology we have: the way you receive your communication from God. There are two ways you receive communication from God.

One is a called a Seer, which is another name for a prophet. The Seer's main prophetic technology is in his / her *eyes*.

The second is a prophet. The prophet's main prophetic technology is *sound and hearing*.

There are some people, like Samuel, who operate from what is called a hybrid anointing, which is called a seer-prophet. Not all seer-prophets are created equal. While some experience vivid visions, others hear clear pronouncements. One method will always be stronger, defining their unique prophetic style. You will go through seasons of each one being sharpened. You will go through seasons of each one being sharpened. Samuel was raised up in the house of Eli and trained by God with hearing his voice at a young age to become a judge, overseeing the school of prophets and anointing kings.

The purpose of pursing your process is to edify, comfort and exhort the body, but also to build and equip the church. To be able to stand and be the light in the midst of all the darkness taking place in the world until Christ returns for His bride. But also, to build an intimate relationship with the Father and become a vessel of honor.

This is why pursing your process and taking the Lord's hand and walking into the greatest journey of your life is important. The reality is, we are all called to prophesy, but we are not all called to walk into the office of a prophet. If you feel that you may be called to the office of the prophet, allow me to invite you to go deeper and ask God to reveal this to you by confirming *"THE CALL"*.

MEDITATION FOR THOUGHT:

1. *What excuses have you made that have kept you from answering the call?*
2. *Reflect on your initial encounter that you had when God first called you. List the different things God brings to your mind or spirit man.*
3. *Has Jesus been calling you to step out and take his hand?*
4. *What is the word, scripture, vision, or dream where God has shown, spoken, or expressed your call? Write it down and keep it before your eyes to build Hope, belief, trust, and faith in God until it manifests.*

_____

_____

_____

_____

_____

_____

_____

_____

Are you a Prophet?

Introduction

Scripture: Numbers 12:6

Thesis: Everyone is called to prophesy, but not everyone is called to the office of a prophet.

i. **The Call to Prophecy**
   - **Personal Encounter:** God's direct call and confirmation.
   - **Overcoming Obstacles:** Addressing fears, doubts, and limitations.
   - **Jeremiah's Example:** God's preparation and empowerment of a prophet.

ii. **Understanding the Prophetic Calling**
   - **The Seer and the Prophet:** Different methods of receiving prophetic communication.
   - **The Hybrid Anointing:** Combining seer and prophet abilities.
   - **The Purpose of Prophecy:** Edification, comfort, exhortation, and building the church.

iii. **The Process of Becoming a Prophet**
   - **Yielding to God's Call:** Surrendering to God's guidance and timing.
   - **Building Trust and Faith:** Developing a deep relationship with God.

- **Receiving God's Words:** Learning to hear and understand God's voice.
  iv. **Confirmation of the Call**
      - **Personal Confirmation:** God's direct revelation and confirmation.
      - **The Journey of Faith:** Trusting God's plan and purpose.
      - **The Rewards of Obedience:** The blessings and fulfillment that come from following God's call.

Questions for the Class:

1. What excuses have you made that have kept you from answering the call?
2. Reflect on your initial encounter that you had when God first called you.
3. List the different things God brings to your mind or spirit man.
4. Has Jesus been calling you to step out and take his hand?
5. What is the word, scripture, vision, or dream where God has shown, spoken, or expressed your call? Write it down and keep it before your eyes to build Hope, belief, trust, and faith in God until it manifests.

ARE YOU A PROPHET

PREPARE FOR WARFARE

The God who gives us peace is also the God who defeats the Enemy in the battle. God will keep his Word of—Satan will not win

— GENESIS 3:15

*"Daughter, Do not lay down your sword to lap up water in this **S-e-a-s-o-n!!**"*

As I sat at my desk contemplating the words resounding in the atmosphere and spent time and prayer seeking God's heart and what He meant by those words, "Daughter do not lay down your sword to lap up water in this season!!"

I realized I had gotten complacent and stopped asking, seeking, and knocking like I once to did. I allowed what was taking place around me to cause me to become distracted. My focus had shifted. I lost sight of what God was doing in my life, and focused on what the enemy was doing instead. I was so engulfed in the situation I couldn't see the solution, let alone seek God or even hear his voice.

My mind went back and forth to the word that was spoken to me earlier that day. As I got up from my desk to go walk for lunch I heard the word again, but it was more personal this time.

"Malinda! Do not put down your sword to lap up water... Do not put down what you have learned over the years. Pick up the word of God. Do not lay down for the enemy. When things get tough, fight the good fight of faith. Now pick up your sword and watch me move!!"

Have you ever laid down your sword to take a break from the warfare? Have you become busy and easily distracted? Have you become complacent about where you are in your life?

We have to first admit that we are in a battle of some sort and recognize who the battle is with and what kind of attack we are experiencing.

WHAT IS SPIRITUAL WARFARE?

Spiritual warfare is defined as a battle against Satan, which takes place in the unseen, spiritual dimension and it's fought with the weapons that have divine power to demolish strongholds, all while you are resisting Satan, standing firm in the faith, remaining strong in the Lord, and pursuing the ultimate victory of demolishing arguments against the knowledge of God and taking captive every thought to make it obedient to Christ.

> *For we do not wrestle against flesh and blood, but against the rulers, against the authorities, against the cosmic powers over the present darkness, against the spiritual forces of evil in the heavenly places.*
>
> — EPHESIANS 6:12

> *Be sober minded; be watchful. Your adversary the devil prowls around like a roaring lion, seeking someone to devour.*
>
> — 1 PETER 5:8

> *Submit yourselves therefore to God. Resist the devil, and he will flee from you.*
>
> — JAMES 4:7

WHAT IS YOUR SPIRITUAL SWORD?

Our spiritual sword is the word of God. To understand the connection between the sword and the word of God, it is important to understand the power of God's word.

> *For the word of God is alive and active. Sharper than any double-edged sword it penetrates even dividing soul and spirit, joint and marrow, it judges the thoughts and attitudes of the heart.*
>
> — HEBREWS 4:12

So, it is important not to lack knowledge of God's word, so that we will not struggle to fight against the enemy. Jesus used God's word as an offensive weapon in Matthew 4 when Satan tried to test him in the wilderness.

While dealing with all the distractions and issues of life, it's not always easy to pick up our swords and fight against the enemy. I've got news for you we are not called to do it on our own strength, but in God's strength.

Life can feel like a constant battle, right? Obstacles pop up, setbacks knock you down, and negative voices whisper doubts. Maybe you're even facing a loss that feels heavy right now. It's easy to wonder, "How do I win this fight?"

The good news is, you don't have to go it alone. In Him, you have a source of strength that can overcome any challenge. But how do you tap into that power and find victory in the midst of spiritual warfare?

Five steps to obtaining victory over spiritual warfare:

1. *Putting on the full armor of God.*
2. *The helmet of salvation and the sword of the spirit are used by renewing our minds in the word or sword of the spirit. This helps to keep us from being influenced in our thoughts or desires. The truth will help us to throw off our old Sinful nature and former ways of life and step into the truth and guard us from the lies of the enemy.*
3. *Coming into agreement with what Jesus has already done for us through the cross and acknowledging that Jesus died for us, and the enemy was defeated.*
4. *Use your shield of faith in front of you as if you were shielding a blow from the enemy. We go forth in faith because we know that God is with us and has gone before us.*

5. *Through prayer, fasting, and supplication we will see the victory.*

You may be in the mist of warfare right now. In the world, we go through warfare, and trials but with Christ will bring us through. Just image if David had given into his fears or insecurities when he went to fight Goliath. Would he have experienced the same outcome? Let's take a look at 1 Samuel 17:41-52 Good News Translation.

DAVID DEFEATS GOLIATH:

> *The Philistine started walking toward David, with his shield bearer walking in front of him. He kept coming closer, and when he got a good look at David, he was filled with scorn for him because he was just a nice, good-looking boy. He said to David, "What's that stick for? Do you think I'm a dog?" And he called down curses from his god on David. "Come on," he challenged David, "and I will give your body to the birds and animals to eat.*
>
> — 1 SAMUEL 17:41-52 GNT

WHAT'S YOUR GOLIATH THAT HAS BEEN CHALLENGING YOU?

Sometimes life throws a curveball – it might be fear, a health battle, financial woes, career uncertainty, a family struggle, a church issue, or even the worry of making the wrong choice. In those moments, it can feel like these challenges are screaming louder than God, drowning out His word and promises. Maybe you even hear echoes of doubt from past dreams, visions, or prayers.

Giants or spiritual strongholds remind us of our disadvantages and limitations by using hopelessness, discouragement, distractions, intimidation, and irritation to keep us in a place of viewing things from our carnal mindset or point of view. Through the lens they provide us, we see only gloom, doom, and defeat.

Let's look at the next verse and see how David's attitude met the opposition standing in the way of his destiny, purpose, and victory.

> *David answered, "You are coming against me with sword, spear, and javelin, but I come against you in the name of the Lord Almighty, the God of the Israelite armies, which you have defied. This very day the Lord will put you in my power; I will*

> *defeat you and cut off your head. And I will give the bodies of the Philistine soldiers to the birds and animals to eat. Then the whole world will know that Israel has a God, 47 and everyone here will see that the Lord does not need swords or spears to save his people. He is victorious in battle, and he will put all of you in our power.*
>
> — 1 SAMUEL 17:45-46 GNT

David showed us the right way we should react when faced with a giant. His stance was rooted in God, and he knew his authority was in the name of the Lord almighty and not in himself. See, David had the right understanding, mindset, and belief due to God preparing David when he killed both the lion and bear. Because David also experienced and knew that God is powerful and almighty, his trust and faith in God caused him to overcome the white noise that the giant was speaking.

> *Goliath started walking toward David again, and David ran quickly toward the Philistine battle line to fight him. He reached into his bag and took out a stone, which he slung at Goliath. It hit him on*

> *the forehead and broke his skull, and Goliath fell face downward on the ground. And so, without a sword, David defeated and killed Goliath with a sling and a stone! He ran to him, stood over him, took Goliath's sword out of its sheath, and cut off his head and killed him.*
>
> *When the Philistines saw that their hero was dead, they ran away. The men of Israel and Judah shouted and ran after them, pursuing them all the way to Gath[a] and to the gates of Ekron. The Philistines fell wounded all along the road that leads to Shaaraim, as far as Gath and Ekron.*
>
> — 1 SAMUEL 17:49-52 GNT

Just as David was able to see that Goliath was no match or comparison with what God is able to do, God wants you to know that you have the same power and might be fully available to you when your giants come to challenge you!

1. *Believe in God*
2. *Take a step back*
3. *Go to God in prayer*

4. *Ask for what you need in that moment – could be strength, etc.*
5. *He will provide your needs*
6. *Stand firm without giving in*
7. *Know that you have a living God on your side that's with you*

Remember, by faith and endurance, you too can stand firm and resist. The God of our father who ensured David's victory will do the same for you! God is faithful to prepare you for warfare!

ARE YOU READY?

MEDITATION FOR THOUGHT:

1. *What fears, obstacles, or barriers have you faced over your life?*
2. *How has God delivered from those very things?*
3. *Reflect on what Jesus did for you through death, resurrection, and barrel.*
4. *Picture Jesus with his arms open wide standing waiting on you to lay all of the False Evidence that Appears Real has been brought to the cross and laid at his feet, disappearing as you step to take Jesus' hand.*

_____

_____

_____

_____

_____

_____

_____

_____

Prepare for Warfare

Introduction

- **Scripture:** Genesis 3:15
- **Thesis:** We are engaged in spiritual warfare against Satan, and God has equipped us with the necessary tools for victory.

i. **Understanding Spiritual Warfare**
   - **The Enemy:** Satan and his demonic forces.
   - **The Battlefield:** The unseen spiritual realm.
   - **The Weapons:** The Word of God and the full armor of God.

ii. **The Importance of Preparation**
   - **Recognizing the Battle:** Identifying the enemy and the nature of their attacks.
   - **The Power of God's Word:** The sword of the Spirit as a weapon against spiritual forces.
   - **The Full Armor of God:** The protective gear provided by God for spiritual combat.

iii. **Steps to Victory**
   - **Putting on the Full Armor of God:** Understanding and utilizing the components of God's armor.
   - **Renewing the Mind:** Filling your mind with God's Word to resist negative thoughts.

- ○ **Agreement with God's Victory:** Acknowledging Jesus' victory over sin and Satan.
- ○ **Faith as a Shield:** Using faith to deflect the enemy's attacks.
- ○ **Prayer, Fasting, and Supplication:** Seeking God's power through prayer and spiritual disciplines.

iv. **Facing Giants**
- ○ **Identifying Giants:** Recognizing the spiritual strongholds in your life.
- ○ **David's Example:** Learning from David's encounter with Goliath.
- ○ **The Power of God:** Relying on God's strength and authority.
- ○ **The Victory of Faith:** Overcoming obstacles through faith and perseverance.

Conclusion

- **The Promise of Victory:** God's assurance of victory over spiritual warfare.
- **The Call to Action:** Embracing your role as a warrior for Christ.
- **The Hope of Eternal Life:** The ultimate victory through faith in Jesus Christ.

Questions for the Class:

1. What fears, obstacles, or barriers have you faced over your life?
2. How has God delivered from those very things?
3. Reflect on what Jesus did for you through death, resurrection, and barrel.
4. Picture Jesus with his arms open wide standing waiting on you to lay all of the False Evidence that Appears Real has been brought to the cross and laid at his feet, disappearing as you step to take Jesus' hand.

_____

_____

_____

_____

_____

_____

_____

_____

ARE YOU A PROPHET

THE CALL

God is faithful, who has called you into fellowship with his Son, Jesus Christ our Lord.

— 1 CORINTHIANS 1:9

Ring, Ring, Ring

Ring, Ring, Ring

Ring, Ring, Ring

Did you hear that? I asked my husband if he heard a phone ringing and he gave me the strangest look as if I was crazy and said, "Noooo."

I looked down at my phone to see if it was my phone ringing, but it was not my natural phone that was ringing, it was my spiritual phone that was ringing. I heard a voice that said, "Malinda answer, The Call, God wants to speak with you."

I looked around, and I saw an archangel whispering in my ear. He was tall with white wings, brown hair, and wearing garments of white and gold. I could see the glory of God all around him.

"Who are you?" I asked him.

He stated, "I am Gabriel the messenger angel. God has sent me to bring you before the throne room He has something that He needs to speak to you about."

I went with the angel, and I saw the streets of heaven, which were gold, and we went into a house. The angel told me, "This is your house in heaven." Then we proceeded to the throne room and there were guards guarding the entry. I could barely look at God, but I could hear the worship and praise taking place around the throne room. Before I knew it, I was on my knees and God started speaking to me about who He has called me to be. He spoke the following scriptures over me.

> *Before I formed you in the womb, I knew you [and approved of you as My chosen instrument], And before you were born, I consecrated you [to Myself as My own]; I have appointed you as a prophet to the nations.*
>
> — JEREMIAH 1:5 AMP

> *Then the LORD stretched out His hand and touched my mouth, and the LORD said to me, "Behold (hear Me), I have put My words in your mouth. "See, I have appointed you this day over the nations and over the kingdoms,*
> *To uproot and break down, To destroy and to overthrow, To build and to plant."*
>
> — JEREMIAH 1:9-10 AMP

As God spoke these Scriptures over me, He touched my mouth and it caught on fire. He placed a coal in my mouth, and then I woke-up.

Another powerful prophetic experience unfolded during a worship service. As I worshipped alongside everyone else, my gaze fell upon a woman nearby. A strange sensation washed over me – it was like having X-ray vision. I saw four or five cysts of varying sizes in her womb area. At the same time, a clear message echoed in my spirit: "As she goes home and worships the Lord, he is going to heal her body fully. When she goes to the doctors, she will have a clean bill of health."

Overcome with excitement at God's work, I felt a surge of heat course through my body. Unable to contain myself, I approached the young lady and embraced her. The warmth radiated from both of us – a tangible confirmation of God's presence. In that moment, I knew with unwavering faith that He had healed her.

I remember going home and taking a nap after the church service. Gabriel, the archangel, came to see me in my sleep.

"I have a room that you need to see." he said. I went with Gabriel to a room in heaven and there was an angel behind the counter asking me what it was that I needed. When I looked down on the counter there was a leg, kidneys, lungs, and a few other body parts the angel had pulled from the rack behind him. I remember seeing eyes, arms, legs, lungs, and many other body parts in this room where the angel handed them out.

I had this experience for three days straight. About a week later I ran into a lady that I have yet to see again. She spoke to me about the healing ministry God had placed down on the inside of me, and I would go from being last to being first, and millions of souls would be healed and come into the kingdom of God. She told me I was a general of God and to keep my hands pure, and my heart, too.

I want to encourage those who have been made to feel crazy, and those who do not believe God can speak to people through dreams and visions.

Dreams and visions aren't just another way for God to get our attention. They're a unique channel through which He can share His will, purpose, plans, and so much more. It's as if He speaks through whispers in the stillness of our sleep, offering healing, deliverance, instructions, and even flashes of inspiration.

Perhaps it's because, amidst the busyness of life – work, family, constant demands – our minds find a deeper state of rest in dreams. In that quiet space, God can pierce through with a message tailored especially for us.

God still speaks to people through dreams and vision, even more today than he has ever done before. I challenge you to seek God about your dreams and visions and do not just write them off as the food you ate the night before. Please understand, God desires to communicate with His people. Dreams and visions are just one way of getting our attention.

Do you believe you can dream again? Do you believe supernatural things still happen? Do you believe God can still inspire hope? Do you believe that God still speaks? Can you dream with God as you once did as a child?

Yes, God still speaks the same way today as he spoke to those in the Bible. For those of you that will second guess or question, let's look at scriptural examples where God spoke. But also, where he said these are the ways that he will pour out his Spirit on us.

> *And it shall come to pass afterward, that I will pour out my Spirit upon all flesh; and your sons and your daughters shall prophesy, your old men shall dream dreams, your young men shall see visions and upon the servants and upon the handmaids in those days I pour out me spirit.*
>
> — JOEL 2:28,29

> *In the last days it shall be, God declares, that I will pour out my Spirit upon all flesh. God's Purpose is to Empower His People in the Last Days. The point is this: in the last days—the days that began with the coming of Jesus—God's purpose is to*

empower his people again and again with extraordinary outpourings of the Spirit, until the witness to his name has reached all the peoples—to the end of the earth.

— ACTS 2:17

We also see in the New Testament where Joseph sees an angel in a dream who warns him to flee to Egypt before Herod can take the life of his son - *Matthew 2:13*. This dream served as a warning.

Pontius Pilate's wife (New Testament) When Jesus stands at trial with Pontius Pilate, his wife warns Pilate against having anything to do with him, because she knows of his innocence - *Matthew 27:19*. The dream informed her about the true nature of Jesus.

These are just a few examples where God spoke through dreams and visions in the bible. Dreams and visions are used to build a closer relationship and intimacy with God. It is like digging for gold or hidden treasures in the earth. Dreams and visions are also like taking symbols and decoding them to understand the message or visions that God gives us, which cause us to seek God the more to gain the understanding of the message that God is trying to convey to his people.

In conclusion, God is still the same yesterday, today and tomorrow. God still speaks through people, dreams, and visions to accomplish his purpose, plans, will and destiny on the earth and through His people.

AND NOW IT IS YOUR CHOICE TO ANSWER THE CALL

MEDITATION FOR THOUGHT:

1. *How does Joel 2:28, 29 speak to you?*
2. *Can you identify how God speaks to you?*
3. *What has kept you from stepping out in faith?*

The Call

Introduction

- **Scripture:** 1 Corinthians 1:9
- **Thesis:** God still speaks to His people through dreams and visions, and it's important to listen and respond to His call.

i. **The Power of Dreams and Visions**
   - **A Unique Channel of Communication:** Dreams and visions as a direct way for God to speak.
   - **Healing and Deliverance:** The transformative power of God's messages.
   - **Instructions and Inspiration:** Guidance and direction from God.

ii. **God's Desire to Communicate**
   - **A Personal Connection:** God's longing to connect with His people.
   - **The Last Days Revival:** God's promise to pour out His Spirit on all flesh.
   - **Biblical Examples:** Examples of God speaking through dreams and visions in the Bible.

iii. **The Importance of Listening**
   - **Building Intimacy:** Dreams and visions as a tool for deepening your relationship with God.

- **Understanding God's Messages:** Deciphering and interpreting God's messages.
- **Seeking God's Guidance:** Seeking God for clarity and understanding.

iv. **Answering the Call**
- **The Choice is Yours:** Deciding whether to respond to God's call.
- **The Rewards of Obedience:** The blessings and fulfillment that come from following God.
- **The Invitation to Step Out:** A challenge to embrace your calling and trust God.

QUESTIONS FOR THE CLASS:

1. How does Joel 2:28, 29 speak to you?
2. Can you identify how God speaks to you?
3. What has kept you from stepping out in faith?

_____

_____

_____

_____

_____

BREAKING OFF THE SPIRIT OF SELF-REJECTION

As you come to him, the living Stone—
rejected by humans but chosen by God
and precious to him.

— 1 PETER 2:4

I can remember sitting on the side of my bed and the eco of my stepdad's voice saying, "No man will ever love you and your husband will only control you."

As he left out of my room and as he proceeded to walk down the stairs to fix himself a drink of crown royal after committing such disgusting act on a child. I remember bawling up in the center of my bed, crying and praying asking God, "Why... why me."

All I wanted to do was become a bird and fly away like the Lenny Kravitz song. Many guys admired me from a far but would never try to talk to me because I was considered mean, hard, and a stuck-up person. Most girls end-up having multiple sexual partners, going from relationship to relationship, but it seemed like I was going in the opposite direction. I would not give a guy the time of day let alone allow anyone to touch me. I became hyper focused on school, working, and taking care of my dad.

This very word curse caused me to go into cycle of self-rejection and all the under linking spirits that were attached to the spirit of rejection. As I got ready to move away for college, I told my uncle that I did not want to get married nor have children. I wanted to get my tubes tied. My uncle told me that one day I would change my mind. Boy, was he right about that.

I never really understood the impact of that word curse was spoken over my life until now. I never realized how difficult I was to love due to me walking in the spirit of rejection, or should I say self-rejection. I knew I would never find true love due me receiving a false report of the enemy. I was told about 4- or 5-years prior that I had herpes, and and my history with cysts, I needed to consider not having children at all.

During my undergraduate years of college, I met a doctor who decided to become a dentist and told me that she did not believe I had herpes, and that I had been misdiagnosed. I went back to the dentist, and she told me I did not have herpes and the test had come back negative.

In the midst of all of this, I had met this really nice guy and I did not want to hide anything from him. So, I told him what happened with another gentleman I was dating and his response shocked me. He said he didn't care about that and wanted to get to know me for me. He even kissed my hand. I could not believe it and was taken aback by his actions.

God used him to show me someone could love and desire to be with me despite all the thing the enemy tried to do in my life. God showed me that I did not have to walk around mourning or wearing sackcloth for clothes. I am thankful for God placing him into my life because the day we said, "I do" was the day the curse was broken off of me and my generations.

The memory flickered back, vivid and raw. It wasn't just the cruel words themselves, the ones my stepfather had branded into me as a young girl: "No man will ever love you and your husband will only control you." It was the way they felt – a heavy black belt wrapped tight around my spirit, suffocating and constricting.

But in that moment, at my wedding altar, something shifted. It was as if, during worship, a transformation unfolded. I remember seeing those words fall away from me, like the unbuckling of a suffocating belt. When I turned to the people around me, a wave of clarity washed over me. The black weight that had bound me for so long lay shattered on the ground, powerless and broken.

I praise God that those words have been broken off of me.

That day wasn't just about the shattering of those specific lies. It was a domino effect of liberation. Many other generational curses, once heavy burdens, were broken off me as well.

Marriage, of course, brings its own challenges. But the tools I received during that powerful encounter – prayer, fasting, and unwavering faith in God's promises – became my armor. As difficulties arose in our marriage, I leaned heavily on those tools. Every word of encouragement God had spoken to me in prayer, every truth gleaned from scripture, became a guiding light, leading us through the storms.

God has given me rest and peace to move forward in Him knowing He causes everything to work together for the good of those who love God and are called according to His purpose for them - *Romans 8:28*.

How about you? Have you ever felt unworthy of being loved? Or like me where you left in awe the first time someone showed interest in you?

Self-rejection can be a major blockage that stops-up the wells of living waters God has placed inside of us. That spirit will cause us to reject the very things God has for us, due to not knowing our self-worth and value.

Deep within us lives a truth whispered by our Creator: we were built for connection. God designed us to thrive in relationships, to find belonging and support in the warmth of a spiritual family.

God used my marriage and children to restore me back to him and as I leaned into God, he unstopped the wells of living waters so that they would flow freely and not be stopped up by demonic forces or ungodly interferences.

The scripture says, "If you knew the gift of God and who it is that asks you for a drink, you would have asked him, and he would have given you living water." - John 4:10.

Through my leaning into God, I was able to touch the hem of his garment and received what I needed to be free.

God is still breaking strong holds and calling us into an intimate relationship today just as he called many different people in the bible to experience the power and love of the Father and He is still moving in this capacity or even greater today.

MEDITATION FOR THOUGHT:

1. *What are the areas of your life that you have felt unworthy?*
2. *Think back to a time where you had no hope but in the midst of this time you were able to see hope and Romans 8:28?*
3. *Have you forgiven yourself?*

If not, take a moment and forgive yourself and ask the Holy Spirit to come to fill those places. You will feel the rivers of living water flow through you and in you.

_____

_____

_____

_____

_____

_____

_____

_____

_____

BREAKING OFF THE SPIRIT OF SELF-REJECTION

Introduction

- **Scripture:** 1 Peter 2:4
- **Thesis:** Self-rejection can hinder our relationship with God and prevent us from experiencing His love and blessings.

i. **The Impact of Self-Rejection**
    - **Blocked Wells of Living Waters:** Self-rejection can prevent us from receiving God's blessings.
    - **Rejection of God's Plans:** Self-rejection can lead us to reject God's purpose for our lives.
    - **The Desire for Connection:** Our innate need for relationships and belonging.
ii. **God's Love and Acceptance**
    - **The Gift of God:** God's unconditional love and acceptance.
    - **The Invitation to Drink:** God's offer of living water.
    - **The Power of Touching the Hem of His Garment:** Experiencing healing and restoration through faith.

iii. **Breaking Free from Self-Rejection**
   - **God's Transformative Power:** God's ability to break strongholds and heal wounds.
   - **The Call to Intimacy:** God's invitation to a deeper relationship with Him.
   - **The Healing Power of Forgiveness:** Forgiving ourselves and others as a path to freedom.

iv. **Experiencing God's Love**
   - **The Flow of Living Waters:** The experience of God's love and grace.
   - **The Restoration of Hope:** Finding hope and purpose in God.
   - **The Invitation to Embrace God's Love:** Accepting God's love and allowing it to transform your life.

Questions for the Class:

1. What are the areas of your life that you have felt unworthy?
2. Think back to a time where you had no hope but in the midst of this time you were able to see hope and Romans 8:28?
3. Have you forgiven yourself? If not, take a moment and forgive yourself and ask the Holy Spirit to

come to fill those places. You will feel the rivers of living water flow through you and in you.

UNSHAKEABLE FAITH

I am the vine, you are the branches; he who abides in Me and I in him, he bears much fruit, for apart from Me you can do nothing.

— JOHN 15:5

I sat nervously in the waiting room, waiting to be called back to see the doctor for my follow-up visit. The nurse opened the door, and stepped out and said, "M-a-l-i-n-d-a - M. H-a-r-r-i-s."

As she paused, she confirmed my birth date and then said, "Follow me... Step on the scale please."

"Yes, ma'am." I replied, and stepped on the scale.

"Looks like you have you have lost a few pounds," the nurse stated as she led me in the room. "Take a seat on the bed or the chair make yourself comfortable until the doctor comes in to see you."

The doctor walked briskly in and said optimistically, "Hi Mrs. Harris! How are you feeling today?"

"I am feeling pretty good;" I answered. Truthfully, I was feeling a little nervous. Before the doctor could tell me the test results, I heard from Holy Spirit, "You have leukemia." It seemed difficult for the doctor to tell me what the results were.

The doctor looked at me and said, "Malinda you have might have leukemia, but I want to make sure." My heart sank I was confused for a few minutes and then I heard the Holy Spirit say, " Don't receive the report from the enemy."

He said, "Cast it down and only speak what God has already spoken about you." I began to confess my faith out loud. It was as if my doctor and I were going toe to toe so, she backed down a bit by asking me to allow her to run a few more tests. I agreed to take the tests, but stood on what God had already spoken to me earlier that day. I had already been healed because of what Jesus did for us on the cross, through His burial, and resurrection. Jesus bore all of our past, present, and future infirmities.

I heard the Holy Spirit say," You will have a clear bill of health. They will not find any traces of leukemia in your body." So, I went to the lab, as instructed by the doctor, and left the hospital with my head held high, knowing God had given me a word to stand on. God was stretching my faith in a major way. Two weeks later, I went back to the doctor's office to receive the report that the Holy Spirit had confirmed in my heart two weeks prior.

Later on, that night a close friend invited me to go see a well-known prophetic voice. During praise and worship, the prophetic minister began speaking about a woman who had been healed from leukemia. He asked for the woman to come forward and share her testimony. His eyes meet my eyes, but I was not ready to get up and share my testimony in front of hundreds of people in the convention center that night. I am thankful that he did not keep pressing the issue or the point. God confirmed two things that night. The first thing was that I had heard his voice. The second was that God had healed me.

Have you ever felt uncertain about your faith? Have you experienced a shaking in your faith? Is God stretching your faith in a new way of putting the word into action?

Exercising our faith is a major key to walking in the kingdom of God. Just as we exercise to get fit, we have to do the same with our faith. It is like lifting weights in the spirit.

As we overcome the different setbacks, trials, and tribulations that we experience in our lives, It causes our faith to increase from faith to faith. Faith is a currency of heaven used to unlock healing, deliverance, understanding, revelation, knowledge, and so much more.

WHAT IS UNSHAKEABLE FAITH?

Faith, by the definition provided in the New Strong's Concordance, is confidence in the testimony of another. Faith is trust, confidence in or assurance. Faith is an active trust in God. It is a belief in what he says is true and it results in action.

> *Now faith is the substance of things hoped for,*
> *the evidence of things not seen. For by it*
> *the elders obtained a good report.*
> *Through faith we understand that the*
> *worlds were framed by the word of God,*
> *so that things which are seen were not*
> *made of things which do appear.*
>
> — HEBREWS 11:1-3

Unshakeable means to be utterly firm and unwavering. So, unshakeable faith means to be grounded and steadfast, and in no way moved away from the hope of the Gospel which you heard, which was preached to every creature under heaven *Colossians 1:21-23*. My definition of unshakeable faith is unmovable trust in what God has spoken, no matter what the situation or outcome looks like in the natural.

The one thing that I want you to catch is that having faith is not being in deception or denial.

> *Faith comes by hearing, and hearing by the word of God.*
>
> — ROMANS 10:17

The word of God is the written word or logos, and the Rhema word is when God speaks to us personally and it's an instant word or vision. When God speaks a word to you, he is revealing his perfect will, plans or purpose for your life, which is what has already been established in heaven and needs to be manifested on earth or in our bodies, for example. We were created in the image of God – *Gen. 1:27*, so that means we have the same creative power as God does because we are created in his image. That means that through sonship and Jesus Christ, God has given us delegated authority and creative power to speak his mind and see the manifestation of those words that have been spoken on God's behalf through you.

HOW DO I ACCESS UNSHAKEABLE FAITH?

1. *Ask God to increase your faith – John 15:7*
2. *By hearing or seeing the word of God – Romans 10:17*
3. *Believing every word that God speaks or shows you – Genesis 28:15*
4. *Step out of your comfort zone – 2 Corinthians 5:7*
5. *Increasing your trust in God – Proverbs 3:5-6*
6. *By allowing your faith to be stretched or increased by being the light – Matthew 5:16, 1 Thessalonians 5:11*

Asking God to increase your faith is done through prayer. As you pray or have a conversation with God, this invites God into our lives and helps us to establish a deeper trust in God. Watch your faith grow stronger and stronger.

Mark 11:23 tells us to pray without doubt in our hearts and believe it will come to pass. In this same passage, Jesus says that if we do this, it will be done for us.

By hearing or seeing, the word of God is done by reading the Bible, Rhema word straight from heaven, or dreams or visions. As we hear or see, the word increases our faith. God confirms his word, and it will never fall to the ground. It will come to pass and we will reap if we faint not.

Our belief system plays a large part in whether or not we trust God. Our belief system is made by our experiences, inferences, and deductions, or by accepting what others tell us to be true. Most of our core beliefs are formed when we are children. Another definition of a belief system is the stories we tell ourselves to define our personal sense of reality. Every human being has a belief system that they use, and it is through this mechanism that we individually "Make Sense" of the world.

The set of beliefs that they have about what is right and wrong and what is true or false. Biblically belief system is the state of the mind when we consider something true even though we are not 100% sure or able to prove it. Beliefs are a choice. We have the power to choose our beliefs and what we come into agreement with or not.

So, we have the choice to believe every word that comes out of the mouth of God. As we see in Gen.28:15, God says, Behold, I am with you and will keep you wherever you go and will bring you back to this land; for I will not leave you until I have done what I have promised you."

How can we not believe, or trust God given that he said I will be with you and complete what I have promised you. That is where we must stay in the word of God to know and understand what God has said and promised us in his word. God will also give you a rhema word, dream, or vision to show you as well that he has not forgotten you and to remind you of what he has promised you. I call those nods and winks from God to keep our faith, hope, belief system, and trust anchored in him alone.

Walking out these 6 steps will increase your faith by leaps and bounds as you come out of your bubble and partner with God, the Lord, and the Holy Spirit you will walk in unshakeable faith to the same degree as the Old Testament prophets and new testament apostles such as Enoch, Elijah, Elisha, Samuel, Deborah, Matt, Luke, John, Peter, and Paul, to name a few.

As you cultivate your relationship with the Holy Spirit you will see God move in a deeper way.

ARE YOU LISTENING AND STEPPING OUT IN UNSHAKEABLE FAITH?

MEDITATION FOR REFLECTION:

1. *When is the last time you have heard a word from God, the Holy Spirit or Jesus?*
2. *If you don't hear, when is the last time you saw a word such as a dream or vision.*
3. *If it's been a while, ask God to increase your faith and willingness to obey him by stepping out into unshakable faith.*

_____

_____

_____

_____

_____

_____

_____

_____

_____

Unshakeable Faith

Introduction

- **Scripture:** John 15:5
- **Thesis:** Unshakeable faith is essential for overcoming challenges and experiencing God's blessings.

i. **Understanding Unshakeable Faith**
    - **Definition:** Unshakeable faith is unwavering trust in God's promises.
    - **The Power of Faith:** Faith is a currency of heaven that unlocks spiritual blessings.
    - **The Biblical Foundation:** The importance of faith as revealed in Scripture.

ii. **Building Unshakeable Faith**
    - **Asking God for Increased Faith:** Praying for a stronger faith.
    - **Hearing and Seeing God's Word:** Engaging with the written and spoken word of God.
    - **Believing God's Promises:** Trusting in God's promises and plans.
    - **Stepping Out of Your Comfort Zone:** Challenging yourself to trust God in new ways.

- **Increasing Your Trust in God:** Cultivating a deeper relationship with God.
iii. **The Role of the Holy Spirit**
    - **The Empowerer:** The Holy Spirit as the source of strength and power.
    - **Cultivating a Relationship with the Holy Spirit:** Seeking intimacy with the Holy Spirit.
    - **The Holy Spirit's Guidance:** Following the guidance of the Holy Spirit.
iv. **The Benefits of Unshakeable Faith**
    - **Overcoming Challenges:** Faith as a tool for overcoming obstacles.
    - **Experiencing God's Blessings:** Receiving the blessings of God through faith.
    - **Walking in God's Power:** Operating in the supernatural power of God.

Conclusion

- **The Invitation to Embrace Faith:** A call to cultivate unshakeable faith in God.
- **The Promise of Victory:** The assurance of victory through faith.
- **The Call to Action:** Stepping out in faith and trusting God's promises.

Questions for the Class:

1. When is the last time you have heard a word from God, the Holy Spirit or Jesus?
2. If you don't hear, when is the last time you saw a word such as a dream or vision.
3. If it's been a while, ask God to increase your faith and willingness to obey him by stepping out into unshakable faith.

_____

_____

_____

_____

_____

_____

_____

_____

_____

_____

_____

_____

ARE YOU A PROPHET

DIG DEEPER

◈

*And he said, "This is what the LORD says:
This dry valley will be filled with pools of
water!*

— 2 KINGS 3:16

One of my brothers in the Lord spoke this word over me 6 months ago. "I have given you the wells of old and new, but you must dig deeper to tap into the new streams, rivers, and oceans I want to unlock deep down on the inside of you, but you must dig deep."

I have been digging in the old wells and new wells that God has placed down on the inside of me through prayer. A month later I had a dream where I was walking down a hallway with doors on each side, and a big effectual door was at the end of the hallway waiting for me with no hindrances, but I first had to go through each door as the Holy Spirit led me to survey the things behind the doors He had given to me through the cross.

As I walked through the door of salvation, I saw myself being prayed for and as I went out under the spirit; I was under crystal clear water. As I stayed under, I saw a large white dove ascend upon me. I felt my body go deeper under the water until I saw a grave underneath me.

I woke up to the words, "I am calling you to dig deeper in Me, and come up higher."

I have always questioned my understanding, revelation, and knowledge as if it were not deep enough. As if it was shallow.

What does God mean by saying dig deep? Have you felt a tugging to come up to a place that is unknown? Are you standing in a hallway or doorway questioning why? What fresh streams has God been calling you to?

Let us start off by defining what digging deeper means and why God would challenge us to do so. Dig deep means to make an effort with all of your resources.

Digging deep refers to your ability to look inside yourself and see your potential and using all that you have to reach your goals, to live out your values and to overcome obstacles. It's speaking to your resiliency or your capability to bounce back after a setback that has taken place in your life.

Digging deep is important to challenging behavior for our mindset and how we react and respond to the different circumstances that arise. Other phrases used for digging deeper are, "Examine more carefully, investigate further, and explore further." An idiom for dig deep is to exert oneself mentally or physically.

When life throws challenges your way – moments of doubt, questioning your calling, feeling unqualified, complacency in your faith, or strained relationships – God calls us to dig deeper. This inner wellspring holds the strength, peace, joy, energy, and drive you need to overcome those hurdles.

Digging deeper also requires growth in our mindset, and a willingness to get uncomfortable in order to change, improve, and finish well.

> *Deep calleth unto deep at the noise of thy waterspouts: all thy waves and thy billows are gone over me.*
>
> — PSALMS 42:7 KJV

One benefit of going deeper with God is that we will produce more fruit. The deeper the root the more fruit we produce.

The wicked desireth the net of evil men: but the root of the righteous yielded fruit.

— PROVERBS 12:12

And the remnant that is escaped of the house of Judah shall again take root downward, and bear fruit upward.

— ISAIAH 37:31

5 SIMPLE STEPS TO DIGGING DEEPER:

1. Identify the obstacles that are standing in the way of your potential.
2. Face the challenges head on.
3. Step out in faith while you are dealing with the obstacles and challenges.
4. Apply scripture to your life.
5. Respond to God in prayer.

But be doers of the word, and not hearers only, deceiving yourselves.

— JAMES 1:22

> *Everyone then who hears these words of mine and does them will be like a wise man who built his house on the rock.*
>
> — MATTHEW 7:24

> *But he answered, 'It is written, "Man shall not live by bread alone, but by every word that comes from the mouth of God."'*
>
> — MATTHEW 4:4

As we walk out those five steps to digging deeper, you will be more aware of the obstacles, behaviors, and mindsets you have that are standing in the way of your potential. You will deal with those challenges one by one, and march boldly on to victory!

As you continue to step out in faith by applying the scriptures to your life, you will experience breakthrough and healing in the areas that were once obstacles and challenges.

ARE YOU READY TO DIG DEEP?

Meditation for thought:

1. *Make a list of obstacles that are standing in the way of your potential.*
2. *Face the challenges head on one obstacle at a time.*
3. *Apply scripture to your life. Remember there is scripture to cover every situation in our lives.*

_____

_____

_____

_____

_____

_____

_____

_____

_____

_____

_____

_____

Dig Deeper

Introduction

- **Scripture:** 2 Kings 3:16
- **Thesis:** Digging deeper into our relationship with God is essential for growth, fulfillment, and overcoming challenges.

   i. **Understanding Digging Deeper**
      - **Definition:** Making an intentional effort to explore and develop ourselves.
      - **The Importance of Depth:** The benefits of going deeper in our faith and personal lives.
      - **The Call to Deeper Levels:** God's invitation to delve into the depths of our being.
   ii. **The Benefits of Digging Deeper**
      - **Overcoming Obstacles:** The strength and resilience gained through digging deeper.
      - **Personal Growth:** The development of a deeper understanding of ourselves and God.
      - **Increased Fruitfulness:** The production of more spiritual fruit as a result of deeper roots.
   iii. **Steps to Digging Deeper**
      - **Identifying Obstacles:** Recognizing the challenges that hinder our growth.

- Facing Challenges Head-On: Confronting obstacles with courage and determination.
- Stepping Out in Faith: Trusting God even in the face of uncertainty.
- Applying Scripture: Using God's Word as a guide and source of strength.
- Responding to God in Prayer: Seeking God's guidance and intervention through prayer.

iv. **The Rewards of Digging Deeper**
- Breakthrough and Healing: Overcoming challenges and experiencing transformation.
- A Deeper Relationship with God: Cultivating a more intimate connection with God.
- Increased Effectiveness: Becoming more fruitful and effective in serving God.

Conclusion

- **The Invitation to Dig Deeper:** A call to explore the depths of your relationship with God.
- **The Promise of Growth:** The assurance of personal and spiritual growth through digging deeper.
- **The Call to Action:** Taking the steps necessary to dig deeper in your faith.

Questions for the Class:

1. Make a list of obstacles that are standing in the way of your potential.
2. Face the challenges head on one obstacle at a time.
3. Apply scripture to your life. Remember there is scripture to cover every situation in our lives.

MALINDA M. HARRIS

TRUST IS A KEY

*Trust in the Lord with all your heart and
lean not on your own understanding; in
all your ways submit to him, and he will
make your paths straight.*

— PROVERBS 3:5-6

"Malinda!" I heard a voice say as I was sitting at my desk listening to worship music and reviewing my work. I looked around, and no one was there, just me.

"Malinda!" I went into a vision of Jesus handing me a beautiful goblet made from gold with red, yellow, blue, and green stones in the center of the cup. It looked like a goblet that kings or queens would drink from.

I heard Jesus say, "Will you drink from this cup?"

I looked around and rubbed my eyes and said, "Huh?"

"Malinda! Will you drink from this cup for your brothers and sisters in me? I remember sitting at my desk crying asking the God the very question the Lord asked God in the garden of Gethsemane, "Let this cup pass from me" Matthew 26:39 I asked three times and all three times God told me **NO!** My grace is sufficient for all your needs.

I finished my work for that day and proceeded home to share what I heard with my family. They all told me, "No, do not drink from that cup."

The question that was asked, "Was the water dirty and murky? If so, it is not a good thing to drink from that cup."

I later learned that it was an assignment God had for me to accomplish with the assistance of the Lord and the Holy Spirit through prayer.

The next day, as I was walking from the parking lot to the building to clock-in, I heard the Holy Spirit say that trust is a key. "I will lead and guide you through this assignment with flying colors and into victory, over the plots and plans of the enemy."

Faced with a difficult choice, I hesitated. The cup before me represented my first prayer assignment – praying for my boss. Memories of being yelled at for asking for work flooded back. A part of me wanted revenge, but a stronger feeling, the Holy Spirit, nudged me towards compassion.

I took a deep breath and drank. I remembered the water in the cup. Smooth on the way down, it turned sour in my stomach, almost like swallowing a scroll. This mirrored the conflicting emotions within me. But ultimately, I decided to drink, to pray for my boss despite my reservations. But then, the Holy Spirit nudged me. What if my boss was hurting too? The unknown of her struggles outweighed my personal resentment.

So, I begin to pray for her and as I did, God allowed me to be a listening ear for her. She was confided in me several different challenges she had encountered and experienced over her last 2yrs of being my boss before she left the company. It was an honor to speak into her life and help her increase her faith and trust in God. It was a humbling experience to pray for her and her family. God opened a great and effectual door for her and her family. They moved to start a new career and her husband opened his own business in a new state. God put everything in order for them. I am thankful I yielded to my assignment through prayer and fasting on their behalf.

Did you know that trust is a key to the kingdom of God? Has God ever presented you with an assignment you wanted to pass over you? Has God asked you to drink from this cup? Can you lay aside your pride and trust God through the process? Would you drink from the cup on behalf of another?

Trust is the foundation of our faith in God's kingdom. The more we trust Him, the stronger our faith becomes. This, in turn, empowers us to take action and live out our beliefs.

The biblical meaning of a cup is heart, covenant, resurrection, life, salvation, or redemption, responsibility or calling, God's will, and assignment.

Trust is confidence; a reliance or resting of the mind on the integrity, veracity, justice, friendship, or other sound principle of another person. He that putteth his trust in the Lord shall be safe. Prov.29. Trusting God is the product of faith God grants us (Ephesians 2:8-9).

When we trust God, we are putting our security in Him, believing His promises, and relying on Him regardless of our circumstances.

Faith is not quite the same as trust, though trust is a natural consequence of faith. Trust, as it is used in the Bible, means to have confidence in, place reliance upon, reasonably expect, believe, and entrust.

We are to trust in God and his love to provide what we need —both in this reality and the next. The Bible warns us not to place trust in our money, jobs, possessions, ourselves, or others.

Pride will keep us from trusting God. The scales of pride keep the breath of God or the Holy Spirit from moving freely and providing the air we need to live and move and have our being in Christ Jesus.

HOW TO BUILD TRUST:

1. *We must diligently seek His direction for our lives. We are all created in God's image with a specific purpose different from each other.*
2. *We must choose to trust God and remember that God is in control.*
3. *His ways are not our ways. We must keep an eternal perspective and live according to what God has revealed in the Bible or his word.*
4. *Fervent Prayer. Prayer is God's secret weapon and the key to unlocking His blessings and power.*
5. *Do not be anxious about anything, but in everything by prayer and supplication with thanksgiving let your requests be made known to God. And the peace of God, which surpasses all understanding, will guard your hearts and your minds in Christ Jesus.*

Seeking with all diligence for his direction for your life or on the behalf of another God will revile the specific purpose and direction for our lives. We realize that trust is a choice, and we have no control over the outcome because it has already been written in heaven. As we trust the Lord and the Holy Spirit and step out of our comfort zone in faith, we will notice our faith and trust in the Lord will increase.

The Holy Spirit will began to give you more understanding, revelation and knowledge as you seek the face of the Father, his kingdom, and his righteousness.

Matthew 6:33 assures us God will add and provide the strategies, blueprints, instructions, and the wisdom on how to apply and rightfully divide or judge the visions and dreams you are having so that you would be able to complete the assignments He directs you in.

Trust is the key that unlocks the door to faith, visions, dreams, and intimacy with the Father. As we go boldly before the throne room of grace and have the confidence to speak the words that God has already spoken about our situation, family, jobs, and other circumstances we can trust or rest in our minds that God has everything that concerns us, and we lack in absolutely nothing.

So, I challenge you. To survey the cross and the keys that have been entrusted to you through Christ Jesus.

LOOK AT YOUR KEYS AND SEE IF YOU HAVE USED THE KEY LABELED TRUST?

MEDITATION FOR THOUGHT:

1. *How can you apply Ephesians 2:8-9 to help build more trust in God?*
2. *How does trust look to you?*
3. *When was the last time you unlocked trust through prayer?*

_____
_____
_____
_____
_____
_____
_____
_____
_____
_____
_____
_____
_____

Trust is Key

Introduction

- **Scripture:** Proverbs 3:5-6
- **Thesis:** Trust is essential for a deep relationship with God and experiencing His blessings.

i. **The Importance of Trust**
   - **Foundation of Faith:** Trust as the cornerstone of our relationship with God.
   - **Empowering Action:** Trusting God empowers us to live out our faith.
   - **The Biblical Meaning of Trust:** The various meanings of trust in the Bible.

ii. **Building Trust in God**
   - **Seeking God's Direction:** Seeking God's guidance for our lives.
   - **Choosing Trust:** Making a conscious decision to trust God.
   - **Living According to God's Word:** Aligning our lives with God's principles.
   - **Fervent Prayer:** Communicating with God through prayer.
   - **Overcoming Anxiety:** Trusting God to provide for our needs.

iii. **The Benefits of Trust**
    - **Unlocking Faith:** Trust as a key to unlocking faith and its blessings.
    - **Experiencing God's Love:** Trusting God leads to a deeper relationship with Him.
    - **Receiving God's Provision:** Trusting God for our needs and desires.
    - **Living a Purposeful Life:** Trusting God's direction for our lives.

iv. **The Call to Trust**
    - **Examining Your Keys:** Evaluating your use of the key of trust.
    - **Surveying the Cross:** Remembering the sacrifice of Jesus Christ.
    - **Embracing Trust:** Choosing to trust God in all circumstances.

Conclusion

- **The Invitation to Trust:** A call to trust God wholeheartedly.
- **The Promise of Blessings:** The assurance of God's blessings through trust.
- **The Call to Action:** Taking steps to build trust in God.

Questions for the Class:

1. How can you apply Ephesians 2:8-9 to help build more trust in God?
2. How does trust look to you?
3. When was the last time you unlocked trust through prayer?

_____

_____

_____

_____

_____

_____

_____

_____

_____

_____

_____

_____

A PROPHETIC WORD FOR WHAT IS TO COME!

Commit your work to the Lord, and your plans will be established.

— PROVERBS 16:3

It is my belief that what is coming is going to supersede Pentecost in this season and seasons to come.

You may ask, "What does she mean in this season, and seasons to come?"

Let us look at John the Baptist and Jesus in Matthew 11:1-19. John was the forerunner, a pioneer, and a messenger of God.

In this season, God is sending out the forerunners with a message for the church but also the world.

"Arise and shine, my sleeping giants. I AM shaking the earth. Arise, Arise, and get into the place, position, and proper alignment I have called you to be in. I AM coming back with a vengeance. I AM calling for the dry bones to be my Army. I Am coming back to rule and reign on the earth. I AM bringing heaven down to earth you will see greater miracles, signs, and wonders than I done in my three years on the earth. You will see wickedness begin to be judged and the right sentences will be handed out. I will give people time to repent and deal with their heart issues. I AM cutting the vines of the wickedness in high places and on the seven mountains I AM removing every wicked altar that has been built even back to Adam and Eve."

Recently, in a dream, God gave me a vision of Jesus as an eagle. There were many other smaller eagles Jesus was carrying on His back as we were soaring above the mountains. When He got close to the mountains in the different countries and states, Jesus released us to go on top of the mountain we had been called to and release the words He had placed in our spirits.

The release of the word was like a torrent of fire erupting from our lips. It wasn't the usual flames, but the purest I'd ever witnessed from prophets and prophetic voices. Unlike any fire I'd seen, this one burned with a blue core and a white tip – a clear sign of revelation straight from the Holy Spirit, so pure it repelled evil itself.

As the fire raged, I saw strongholds and towers crumble over cities, replaced by bastions of God's light. A revival unlike any before swept across the United States. The intensity of the fire was unprecedented – four to seven times greater than anything we'd ever seen. This, I knew, would usher us into a new era of unwavering dependence on the Holy Spirit.

You will know that it's God and not man or woman or from the flesh. It will be Holy Spirit inspired and straight from the throne room of God, and from the books in heaven. We will see evangelism like never before. We will see prophets speak, and it will manifest as quickly as we speak it.

God is overturning the spoils of the enemy to Godly and righteous people who will advance His kingdom here on the earth and obey Him down to the letter.

I saw unlimited resources being released to do the work of the Father. We are going into the mightiest harvest that we have ever seen. We will live in the 1000-year rule and reign of Jesus on earth, like in the book of Revelation.

The body of Christ has been under attack in the earthly realm for many centuries, especially the prophetic ministry. The enemy has come in unaware to steal, kill, and destroy. The enemy will wait and look for opportune times when we cannot resist or fight for ourselves against his attacks.

As a prophet and prophetic voice, the Holy Spirit gave me a word about who God says that I am. He showed me the devil is like a roaring loin walking around, seeking whom he may devour. 1 Peter 5:8 The Holy Spirit said to me, "Malinda, look back over your life and see where my goodness, grace, and mercy kept you and how the enemy tried to devour you and sift you like wheat."

Satan's attacks target our potential, destiny, and calling – the very roadmap laid out for us in heaven. God, who knows the end from the beginning, has already inscribed our life stories. Yet, navigating the "middle" – the journey to fulfill that purpose – requires actively seeking Him. It's in this pursuit that we learn to overcome the attacks that threaten to derail our identities, destinies, and callings.

To take it further, the Holy Spirit showed me that our childhood is an opportune time for tares to be planted in the night season through dreams, visions, or everyday life.

It is important for us to put a guard over our hearts with all due diligence. We never look at what is connected to our hearts, such as our mouth, eyes, and ears, which I call gates. As children, this can mean young or old the devil will use our life circumstances to plant tares which can be fear, rejection, doubt, and unbelief or any other demonic force. Movies and TV shows often serve to desensitize us through subliminal messages and plant the opposite of what God intended for us to grow within our hearts and minds.

Imagine our spirits as gardens where seeds are sown, destined to bear fruit. Within God's kingdom, everything begins as a seed. Just as the parable of the wheat and tares shows, the enemy seeks to destroy these seeds. The tares represent external influences that try to choke out the good seeds, the divine purpose God has planted within us.

Recognizing that we are spiritual beings existing in the world, but not of it, empowers us. We are here to fulfill the will, purpose, and plan of the Father, our God.

Due to the devil at one time being an angel in the kingdom of God, he had access to our books of life and knows what God's plan is for each and every one of us. Satan, heard God's conversations about us, and he would do anything to stop what God is doing in our lives to build his army. Satan's reasoning is that he could build a kingdom higher than God's and He wanted to be God. He fell into pride and destruction because of his haughty spirit and deception.

The main reasons why we are under so much demonic attack in the prophetic is because Satan not only has a bone to pick with God, but he wants to prove a point and win as many souls as possible into his kingdom of darkness. Satan feels he is the king of the earth, and this is his throne and not God's.

Another reason why the enemy attacks us is to test the word

and the revelation knowledge we have received from God, whether it be through the written word or Rhema word.

The enemy will test the word to see if we are living out this word in our lives or not. We must not only preach and teach the word of God, but we are called to live the word as a living sacrifice. We win in the end, and today we have the Victory in Christ Jesus.

We are in the last days, and all of this has been written in Revelation. We are living out the prophecies of the end times.

I wanted to share an encouraging word with you that the Lord gave me one time when I was going through an attack from the enemy.

Do not allow the enemy to clothe you in the clothes that God has not clothed you in. We will no longer walk in fear, rejection, doubt, and unbelief. We will put on the clothes that God prepares for us daily.

When we are going through setbacks or are being knocked back, our faith and trust in the Lord is being tested. It is like moving four to six steps forward and being knocked back seven steps by the enemy. Our Faith has been put on public display for everyone to see what kind of pressure we are under, and we will show our true colors.

Challenges offer us the opportunity to endure. Through endurance, we grow, becoming more complete and mature in our responses. This maturity helps us navigate setbacks and avoid getting stuck in them.

Ultimately, God's faithfulness and promises shine through for those who persevere in the fight of faith. By keeping our focus on Him, we rise above our current circumstances and emerge stronger.

We all face challenges that feel overwhelming. But here's the good news: you don't have to face them alone! With God's strength by your side and the joy He brings, you can actually find these trials to be opportunities for growth. As James 1:2-4 NLT says, 'Consider it pure joy, my brothers and sisters, whenever you face trials of many kinds, because you know that the testing of your faith produces perseverance. Let perseverance finish its work so that you may be mature and complete, not lacking anything.'"

God, in His immense love, has gifted us with a piece of Himself - the Holy Spirit. This divine spark within us isn't meant to keep us nestled in comfort. It's the very fuel that empowers us to take flight! Whether your gift lies in the realm of the prophetic, bringing forth messages of hope and guidance, or in another area entirely, God equips you with the tools you need. He invites us to spread our wings, to leave the familiar behind and soar alongside Him on the winds of purpose. Let the Holy Spirit guide you, fulfilling the magnificent destiny He has planned for each of us.

Meditation for thought:

1. *Where is your life, have you allowed the enemy to cloth you?*
2. *What have you done to shift and step into the clothes that God has prepared for you?*
3. *How can you apply James 1:2-4 NLT to your life?*

A Prophetic Word for What is to Come

Introduction

- **Scripture:** Proverbs 16:3
- **Thesis:** A powerful revival is coming, and we must prepare ourselves to be part of it.

i. **The Forerunner**
   - **The Role of the Forerunner:** The messenger preparing the way for God's movement.
   - **The Call to Arise:** The call for God's people to awaken and step into their calling.
   - **The Coming Revival:** The prediction of a greater revival than Pentecost.

ii. **The Vision of the Eagle**
   - **The Symbol of the Eagle:** The eagle representing freedom, power, and vision.
   - **The Release of the Word:** The powerful proclamation of God's message.
   - **The Transformation of Cities:** The destruction of strongholds and the establishment of God's kingdom.

iii. **The Enemy's Attacks**
   - **Targeting Potential, Destiny, and Calling:** Satan's strategies to hinder God's plans for our lives.

- **Planting Tares:** The enemy's attempts to sow seeds of doubt, fear, and unbelief.
- **The Importance of Guarding Our Hearts:** Protecting our hearts from demonic influences.

iv. **The Victory of Faith**
- **Overcoming Challenges:** The power of faith to overcome obstacles.
- **The Enduring Nature of Faith:** The ability of faith to persevere through trials.
- **The Gift of the Holy Spirit:** The empowerment of the Holy Spirit for spiritual growth and victory.

Conclusion

- **The Call to Action:** Preparing ourselves for the coming revival.
- **The Promise of Victory:** The assurance of God's victory over the enemy.
- **The Invitation to Soar:** The call to embrace our spiritual gifts and fly high with God.

QUESTIONS FOR THE CLASS:

1. How can you apply Ephesians 2:8-9 to help build more trust in God?

2. How does trust look to you?
3. When was the last time you unlocked trust through prayer?

For no prophecy was ever produced by the will of man, but men spoke from God as they were carried along by the Holy Spirit.
2 Peter 1:21

AFTERWORD

The first chapter of the book on identity inspired me to focus on my identity and who my identity is found in. Is it my negative past situations of my life or found in Christ who has been my safe refuse and hiding place and who has given me unshakable faith to continue on my life's journey.

As I continued to read the book, the scripture *Philippians 4:13* comes to mind that,

> *I can do all things through Christ who gives me strength.*

I believe this book will help people from all walks of life, step into their true identity and answer the high calling on their lives.

AFTERWORD

Are you a prophet is a great tool for healing, breakthrough, and encouragement to step into your call.

Jamar A. Brown

ABOUT THE AUTHOR

Eagle's Emerge
Rise up!

Malinda M. Harris is a prophetic minister, teacher, and firebrand speaker fueled by a passion to see people rise above life's challenges and fulfill their God-given destinies. Drawing upon her unique background in mechanical engineering (BSME, Alabama A&M University) and her calling as a mouthpiece for God (Isaiah 61 Global Fire Ministries), Malinda equips believers to hear the voice of God and embrace their prophetic callings.

A sought-after speaker at women's ministries, prayer gatherings, and prophetic conferences, Malinda's message ignites hearts to not only overcome personal struggles but also to influence their families, churches, communities, and the world at large. Her training empowers believers to discern God's heart on current and future issues, propelling them into their prophetic destinies.

When Malinda isn't busy serving as a servant of God and a prophetic voice, she enjoys life in Mobile, Alabama with her husband, Jerald, and their three children.

books2read.com/malinda-harris

ABOUT THE PUBLISHER

LAKEVIEW
PUBLICATIONS

"Everyone has a story to tell, only the courageous will find a way to get it told. Let my team and I help you become courageous!"

Helping people become courageous is something we have been doing since LakeView Publications was founded in 2018.

With every author we have helped since book one, I am reminded of the day I decided to take the big step of writing my first book. I was quickly overwhelmed with trying to figure out how to bring my dream to life, I just knew that I had a message to share with the world. If you are like I was, You are *NOT* alone! Nearly 100% of our clients started with an idea but had no idea what to do with their idea. That is where my team and I come in. We publish AMAZING books written by AMAZING people who had an idea and took a step in courage to ask the right question. The best way to start, or at least get the next steps is to ask the most important question.

How Do I Get My Book Published?

Finding the right publisher is key. The team at LakeView Publications is driven by our passion to help people tell their stories and in helping them find a way to allow their story to take them to the next level. One of the greatest parts about assisting people in the publishing journey of their story is being able to connect with them and help them find their voice. You reach out to us with the best way to reach you, and we do the rest. It's that easy!

You wrote the book; we do everything else!

When you contact us, we will find out where you are in the process and give you an assessment of what you will need to get you from where you are to where you want to be!

Our team is absolutely magnificent, and they are dedicated to excellence. We offer proofing, editing, layout design, ghostwriting, art illustration, storyboard layout, content coaching, graphic design, and everything else you may need to get your book published and released.

www.LakeviewPublishers.com

facebook.com/LakeviewPublishing
instagram.com/lakeview_publishing

Want to Publish Your Book?

We Can Help!

* Manuscript Editing

* Book Cover

* Book Formatting

*Illustrations

* Publishing through all major retailers
(Amazon, Kobo, B&N, Apple)

* Paperbacks & eBooks

* Blurb Writing

* Audio Books

* Choose Your Own Package

* Author Retains **ALL** rights

We're here to help!

"Everyone has a story to tell, only the courageous will find a way to get it told. Let my team and I help you become courageous!"

LakEview
PUBLICATIONS

www.LakeviewPublishers.com

Made in the USA
Columbia, SC
09 February 2025

Made in the USA
Columbia, SC
14 February 2025